Master Edition with performance license.

See Permissions for more information.

A Kazoo Christmas

A Comedic Intergenerational Christmas Pageant

Christopher D. Rodkey

Barber's Son Press

York, Pennsylvania

Published by

BARBER'S SON PRESS

York, Pennsylvania

<u>**See Permissions information on the next page.**</u>

© 2023 Christopher D. Rodkey.

ISBN: 978-1-7347188-5-0.

Library of Congress Control Number (LCCN): 2023936771.

Master Edition: includes license to perform in nonprofit settings for twelve months following the date of purchase.

This pageant had its first live performance at St. Paul's United Church of Christ, Dallastown, Pennsylvania, in December, 2021. Special thanks: Dr. Andrea Stephenson.

All music suggested in this production is in the public domain.

10   9   8   7   6   5   4   3   2   1

PERMISSIONS

1. A <u>limited license</u> included with purchase of this edition of *A Kazoo Christmas.*

    A. This **<u>Master Edition</u>** is sold with a license to perform in a nonprofit setting for <u>twelve months</u> following the date of original purchase.

    B. This license allows <u>limited photocopying</u> in conjunction with performances within the twelve-month license.

    C. No part of this play may be digitally copied, shared, or stored without express written permission from the author.

    D. This license does include recording or broadcast rights for one-time non-profit religious use.

    E. All music suggested in this script for use is in the public domain in the United States. The author and publisher accept no liability for use or broadcast of music.

2. <u>Attribution</u> shall be expressed by the license holder as follows:

    A Kazoo Christmas © 2023 Christopher D. Rodkey. Performed under license agreement with Barber's Son Press.

3. <u>Other editions</u> available from the publisher.

    A. **<u>Performer's Manuscript Edition</u>**: a lower-priced, saddle-stitched copy that may be used for one-time performance. This edition does not include the additional materials of this version and only includes the text of the play.

    B. **<u>Library Edition</u>**: hardcover copy identical to the Master Edition intended for educational, academic, or reference use. It does not include a license for performance or permission to copy.

4. <u>Renewal or purchase of additional licenses</u> for performance.

The owner of this edition may purchase a twelve-month license from the publisher. Contact the publisher for further information.

5. <u>Requests for other permissions</u> for use of this play should be directed directly to the author or publisher.

6. <u>Additional music or elements</u> added to this play by the holder of this performance license must seek permission from appropriate authors and copyright holders if the material is not in the public domain.

Contact for the author: cdrodkey@yahoo.com.

TABLE OF CONTENTS

PLAYWRIGHT NOTE

This pageant came from a silly, joking suggestion from a child, after watching the famous "Kazoo Kid" video meme: *Let's have a kazoo Christmas!* And her clergy father thought for a moment and said, "That's not a bad idea!"

"What would a 'kazoo Christmas' be like?" I then asked the child.

The only response was a shrug of the shoulders and assurance that "I think you can figure that out, Daddy."

Challenge accepted.

Three years later, after watching one of my favorite episodes of *The Simpsons*--"Bart Sells His Soul" (season 7, episode 4)-- while sick on Christmas, the ideas for this play coalesced. If my reader is a fan of *The Simpsons,* they will find some gestures and homage in the pageant. Names of characters are "Easter Eggs" that fans of the show will connect.

I intend this play to be easily adaptable for small or large groups, for churches who wish to incorporate adults or teens into various roles for comedic value. The star, for example, could be an older adult, or all of the nativity players could be adults with the children taking on the primary story roles. In like manner, the music could be adapted as appropriate and meaningful to your congregation.

The play is a pageant-within-a-pageant, with a pageant within the play, following an abbreviated version of traditional "Lessons and Carols" liturgies commonly used for Christmas Eve worship. This play could replace or make a respectful parody of your congregation's practice, if or when appropriate.

I also include some Advent candle-lighting liturgies to use in conjunction or in promotion of the pageant. These could be used to involve other laity, adults, parents, or children into the excitement of the season and of the forthcoming pageant.

In terms of theological perspective, I wrote this play to be theologically neutral to be used across many different kinds of churches. I intentionally avoided instances where opportunities to be more denominationally-specific exist in the story (how Mary is addressed, for example). I trust your direction to make sense for your own local worshiping community.

Eastertide, 2023

CHARACTERS

BARTHOLOMEW	An older child or teenager, a jokester.
FILLMORE	An older child or teenager, a jokester. A side-kick to Bartholomew.
ALISA	An older child or teenager; a friend of Bartholomew and Fillmore.
ORGANIST	The church musician or a portrayal of one.
CHILDREN	As many as desired for the community and production, including or in addition to other nativity players.
CHILD #1	A younger child.
CHILD #2	A younger child.
PASTOR	The pastor or portrayal of the church's pastor.
MARY*	Mary, mother of Jesus, in a nativity presentation.
ANGEL(s)*	One or more angels in a nativity presentation.
JOSEPH*	Earthly father of Jesus in a nativity presentation.
ANIMALS*	Miscellaneous animals in the nativity presentation.
MAGI*	Three magi in a nativity presentation.
STAR*	A person in a star costume for a nativity presentation.
SHEPHERDS*	One or more shepherds in a nativity presentation.
BABY JESUS*	A baby or prop baby in a nativity presentation.

*Non-speaking roles.

SETTING

A church; Sunday School classroom, sanctuary.

TIME

Shortly before Christmas Eve. Christmas Eve. The Present.

SYNOPSIS

Alisa greets Bartholomew and Fillmore, who are cleaning the closets of a Sunday School room as punishment for playing a prank on the church organist. The boys discover an old box of kazoos, and immediately come up with a plan to hijack the upcoming Christmas pageant with the kazoos. Alisa refuses to participate.

Later Bartholomew and Fillmore meet with the church children to devise a plan to interrupt the Christmas pageant by playing kazoos during Christmas Carols and acting out what they believe will be a better kind of pageant—with kazoos. Alisa walks in on the meeting and again raises her objections; the boys and the children commit to move forward with their plans.

On Christmas Eve, before the pageant, Bartholomew and Fillmore again meet with the children to review their plans, and Alisa arrives to beg them not to interrupt the pageant. The Pastor walks in on the meeting and reveals that he knows that they are planning to have a "kazoo choir." While asking them to take over the music for the organist, because she is sick, the Pastor becomes visibly ill, and charges Alisa to lead the pageant with the boys and children to provide the music. Stunned, Bartholomew reveals that they didn't think through what a whole pageant would be like in their plans to hijack the service, but Alisa explains that they will lead carols with kazoos just like normal.

Shortly thereafter, the pageant begins. Alisa leads a simple pageant modeled upon the traditional Service of Lessons and Carols. The pageant is successful, but at the end, the children don't know how to properly end it. The Organist then appears and confesses that she set them up to do the pageant when he or she discovered that the boys were conspiring a plan. Bartholomew then addresses the audience, confessing that he was going to hijack the pageant, but God reveals to them gifts that sometimes need redirected.

The play concludes with a ruckus rendition of "Joy to the World" with the organ and kazoos.

ORDER OF MUSIC

All songs suggested in this script are in the public domain.

"Good King Wenceslas"

"O Holy Night"

"Deck the Halls"

"O Christmas Tree"

"Jingle Bells"

"While Shepherds Watched"

"O Come, All Ye Faithful"

"Lo, How a Rose E'er Blooming"

"O Come, O Come, Emmanuel"

"O Little Town of Bethlehem"

"Angels from the Realms of Glory"

"What Child is This?"

"The First Noel"

"We Three Kings"

"Hark! The Herald Angels"

"Angels We Have Heard on High"

"Away in a Manger"

"Silent Night"

"Joy to the World"

A KAZOO CHRISTMAS

ACT I

TIME: The present.
PLACE: A Sunday School
classroom.

Off stage the ORGANIST is
sitting, likely at the
organ.

BARTHOLOMEW and FILLMORE
are cleaning out a closet
when ALISA enters.

ALISA

Walks into classroom.

Bartholomew and Fillmore, what are you doing?

BARTHOLOMEW

Alisa! Fillmore and I are being punished by our parents.

FILLMORE

We have to clean out the closets of the Sunday School rooms.

(Points at BARTHOLOMEW.)

(Accusingly.) It was all Bartholomew's idea!

ALISA

(Laughing.) I heard!

(Pauses.)

Well, *I* thought it was funny when you switched around the organist's music.

BARTHOLOMEW

We needed to get the church moving in their seats a little. I thought they would thank me for spicing up the music a little bit!

FILLMORE

(Sarcastically.) Yeah, right. Like you didn't think anyone would notice that instead of "In the Garden" the organist played "In the Garden of Eden."

BARTHOLOMEW

Oh, I was hoping they'd notice. Mom and Dad didn't think it was very funny.

FILLMORE

It was worth it just to hear the Pastor say, "Wait a minute, this sounds like 'rock and/or roll.'"

ALISA

And here you both are, cleaning out the Sunday School closets.

FILLMORE

Have you ever looked in these church closets before? Cleaning these out is like an archeological expedition!

ALISA

Well, boys, I'll leave you to your punishment. Hope you've learned your lesson: never, *ever*, mess with the church organist.

> *(Points to the ORGANIST and*
> *winks.)*

(Exiting.) Never, *ever*, mess with the church organist.

BARTHOLOMEW

> *(Interrupts ALISA, who stops*
> *when BARTHOLOMEW speaks.)*

Woah! Check it out!

> *(Discovers a box or pulls a box*
> *out of the closet.)*

                              FILLMORE

What is it?

                              BARTHOLOMEW

                    *(Looks into box, and becomes
                    mischievously excited.)*

You are *not* going to believe what I just found!

                              ALISA

Only *you* could be impressed with some old flannelgraph or
videotapes with singing vegetables from, like, the last century.

                              BARTHOLOMEW

(Astonished, and laughing.) Oh, no. Even better.

                    *(Shows the inside of the box to
                    FILLMORE.)*

                              FILLMORE

                    (Looks inside the box, and laughs.)

Bartholomew, this is the *best thing* ever.

                              BARTHOLOMEW

It's not one *thing*, but it's a lot of *things*.

                              ALISA

Now you have me interested. What's in the box?

                              BARTHOLOMEW

(To Filmore.) Fillmore, are you thinking what I'm thinking?

                              FILLMORE

Are you thinking… *best Christmas ever?*

                              BARTHOLOMEW

(Smiling, nodding.) I think this is a moment where the Holy
Spirit is speaking to us from this old Sunday School closet.

                              ALISA

What? What is it?

                           BARTHOLOMEW

It's a whole box full…

              (*Shows FILLMORE and the
              audience that the box full of kazoos.*)

…of kazoos!

                              ALISA

What does *that* have to do with Christmas?

                             FILLMORE

I think this means that *this* year, we're going to have a kazoo
Christmas!

                              ALISA

What does that even mean?

(*Pauses.*)

(*Continues to speak with horror.*) Wait a minute!

(*Accusingly.*) Bartholomew, you're not going to replace the organ
with kazoos Christmas?

(*Pauses.*)

Are you?

                           BARTHOLMEW

Oh, no. *Even better…* Fillmore, what is the most annoying
Christmas song ever?

                             FILLMORE

Hm…

(*Thinking, pausing.*)

I'm going to say that it's… "Good King Wenceslas!"

1   *BARTHOLOMEW takes two kazoos from*
2   *the box, and hands one to FILLMORE.*
3
4   ALISA
5
6 "Good King" *who?*
7
8   BARTHOLOMEW
9
10 "Good King *Wenceslas!*"
11
12
13 MUSIC CUE: "Good King Wenceslas," kazooed by Bartholomew and
14 Fillmore in an exaggerated and intentionally obnoxious way.
15
16
17   ALISA
18
19   *(About 20-30 seconds into the song,*
20   *ALISA covers her ears.)*
21
22 *Stop! Stop!*
23
24   BARTHOLOMEW
25
26   *BATHOLOMEW stops kazooing, while*
27   *FILLMORE continues, clearly enjoying*
28   *the silliness of his performance.*
29
30   *BARTHOLOMEW gestures FILLMORE*
31   *desperately to stop the song.*
32
33 Alisa, don't you know you *never* interrupt an old-fashioned kazoo
34 hoedown?
35
36   ALISA
37
38 *That* … was disturbing.
39
40   FILLMORE
41
42 Oh, just wait until we give "Silent Night" the kazoo treatment!
43
44   ALISA
45
46 *No.* Bartholomew and Fillmore, don't do whatever it is you're
47 thinking about doing.

1   BARTHOLOMEW
2
3   *BARTHOLOMEW stands proudly and*
4   *defiantly.*
5
6   *The time has come, my friends.* We are going to hijack the
7   Christmas Eve service this year and replace it with a "Kazoo
8   Christmas."
9
10   ALISA
11
12 No one is going to allow that.
13
14   BARTHOLOMEW
15
16 If we give a kazoo to each of the little kids in the Christmas
17 Pageant and announce, *(loudly)* "It's time for a 'Kazoo
18 Christmas,'" the children will follow suit.
19
20   ALISA
21
22 Have you ever tried to lead children in anything? Especially
23 around church? It's like herding cats!
24
25   BARTHOLOMEW
26
27 *(Sarcastically.)* Don't be so clichéd, Alisa. It will be like the
28 people wandering through the desert to the Promised Land!
29
30   ALISA
31
32 Bartholomew, are you really going to compare yourself to
33 Moses?
34
35 *(Pauses.)*
36
37 You do know that part of that story is that the Egyptians
38 followed Moses into the Red Sea.
39
40   BARTHOLOMEW
41
42 You're right! Moses was brilliant! That's in the Bible! And
43 that worked out great!
44
45   ALISA
46
47 *(With surprised confusion.)* Um… not for the Egyptians.

                          BARTHOLOMEW

It was so epic, that thousands of years later, we're still
talking about how Moses saved God's people!

                          FILLMORE

(Sarcastically.) And Alisa, aren't *we* God's people?

                          ALISA

Yes, but that's not how the Bible story goes…

                          FILLMMORE

(Interrupts.) You know what? I bet Moses used kazoos!

                          ALISA

Oh, come on! There here aren't any kazoos in the Bible.

                          FILLMORE

Yes, there were! They were call shofars!

                          ALISA

(Shocked and confused.) I don't think that's what shofars are.
                          BARTHOLOMEW

Enough! While you two were going back and forth I prayed on it,
and I have received a moment of clarity!

                          ALISA

(Slaps her head.) Oh, no…

                          FILLMORE

Like Moses descending from the mountain, and the shofar sounded
to God's people…

                          BARTHOLOMEW

(Interrupts, pretentiously.) …We will give the children of God
kazoos, and they will follow the rules as we give them! The
children will listen to us!

                          ALISA

The Pastor and Organist are not going to like this.

FILLMORE

Well, you know, Moses had to break some stuff to get everyone's attention.

ALISA

You two are going to be punished with cleaning out the church storage shed next.

BARTHOLOMEW

But this will be the most memorable Christmas pageant ever.

FILLMORE

Yeah… imagine the strong faith that we will be empowering for the children. It will be better than any children's choir doing a pageant…

BARTHOLOMEW

(Interrupts.) … better than any children's pageant *ever.*

ALISA

I don't want anything to do with this. You two can spend the new year cleaning the shed by yourselves.

BARTHOLOMEW

> *Bartholomew holds a kazoo up to*
> *his forehead, and turns to Fillmore,*
> *who also then holds his kazoo to his*
> *forehead.*

My kazoo sense is telling me that you're going to help us with the "Kazoo Christmas."

ALISA

You can tell your kazoos that *I* will have nothing to do with this.

FILLMORE

(Defiantly.) The *kazoo* says otherwise. Let's get the children!

End of Act I.

1
2
3
4
5
6
7
8
9
10
11

MUSICAL INTERLUDE 1

                         (Between Acts I and II, one or
                         more characters or players will
                         offer a musical piece on kazoo
                         or with a piano or organ.)

MUSIC CUE: "O Holy Night," initial played sincerely and then
played in an exaggerated and noisy way for humor.

<u>ACT II</u>

TIME: The present.

PLACE: A choir rehearsal room or classroom, or in a church sanctuary.

(BARTHOLOMEW and FILLMORE enter and stand in front of the children, as if they are directing them.)

BARTHOLMEW

Children! Who wants to have the best Christmas ever?

CHILDREN

(Shouting individually and corporately.) Me! Us! We do!

FILLMORE

Who wants to have the *best* Christmas *pageant* ever?

CHILDREN

(Shouting individually and corporately.) Me! Us! We do!

BARTHOLOMEW

Children! I am going to bestow upon you the holy office of kazoo player.

CHILD #1

(CHILD #1 raises hand excitedly, stands to speak.)

Does that mean we are getting kazoos?

FILLMORE

We have a *whole box* of kazoos for each and every one of you.

CHILDREN

(Shouting.) Yay!

(FILLMORE hands out kazoos to every child, and then to the audience

> *surrounding the CHILDREN or*
> *the entire audience.)*

                    BARTHOLOMEW

All you all have to do is to kazoo along with me.

MUSIC CUE: Bartholomew kazoos "Deck the Halls" or another
familiar song, and, while playing, encourages the children to
kazoo along with him in a cacophonous and noisy rendition.

                    FILLMORE

That was beautiful.

                    ALISA

          (ALISA walks in.)

What was that?

                    BARTHOLOMEW

(Kazooing-intonating.) < What was what? >

                    ALISA

That awful noise!

                    BARTHOLOMEW

(Kazoo intonating.) < I don't know! >

                    ALISA

Wait a minute. You're really going to go through with taking
over the Christmas pageant? Unbelievable!

                    BARTHOLOMEW

          (Offers ALISA a Kazoo.)

(Kazoo-intoning.) < Here you go! >

                    FILLMORE

What Bartholomew is trying to say is that you're welcome to
join us for what will be the most epic…

1   *(FILLMORE points at the children.)*

2

3   CHILDREN

4

5   *(Loudly kazooing.)* < *WOOO!* >

6

7   FILLMORE

8

9   …Christmas…

10

11   *(Points at the CHILDREN again.)*

12

13   CHILDREN

14

15 *(Loudly kazooing.)* < *WOOO!* >

16

17

18   FILLMORE

19

20 …Pageant…

21

22   *(Points at the CHILDREN again.)*

23

24   CHILDREN

25

26 *(Loudly kazooing.)* < *WOOO!* >

27

28   FILLMORE

29

30 …Ever!

31

32   *(Points at the CHILDREN again.)*

33

34   CHILDREN

35

36 *(Loudly kazooing, louder and longer than previously.)* < *WOOO!*

37 >

38

39   ALISA

40

41 I don't know, I –

42

43   BARTHOLOMEW

44

45   *(BARTHOLOMEW interrupts by*

46   *kazooing.)*

47

48 Alisa, don't be a kazoo scrooge!

MUSIC CUE: Bartholomew kazoos the beginning notes of "O Christmas Tree," and as the Children join in the song, in an exaggerated way, Bartholomew kazoos in Alisa's face, playfully taunting her.

                         FILLMORE

C'mon, Alisa! Live a little! It's Christmas! Can't you imagine the beauty and tenderness of "Silent Night" on kazoo?

            (CHILDREN laugh at FILLMORE's
            joke.)

            (FILLMORE points at the CHILDREN
            again.)

                         CHILDREN

(Loudly kazooing.) < WOOO! >

                         ALISA

            (ALISA hands the kazoo back to
            BARTHOLOMEW.)

Well, the Pastor just asked me to have a part in our Christmas Eve service, so I hope you won't be so rude as to interrupt me!

                         BARTHOLOMEW

I guess we'll find out!

MUSIC CUE: Bartholomew leads a verse of "Jingle Bells" or another festive song on the kazoo and leads CHILDREN or off stage.

End of Act II.

1
2
3

MUSICAL INTERLUDE 2

4 MUSIC CUE: "While Shepherds Watched," on kazoo, optionally
5 with piano or organ. The audience is humorously led by
6 Bartholomew and Fillmore.
7
8 MUSIC CUE: "O Come All Ye Faithful," with similar
9 instrumentation and humor.

ACT III

TIME: The present. Christmastime.

PLACE: A church sanctuary.

BARTHOLOMEW and FILLMORE are standing in front of the children, who may be wearing pageant costumes.

BARTHOLOMEW

(Speaking, as if whispering or hushed, to CHILDREN.) Listen, everybody! We're going to crash the pageant when they start singing "Lo, How a Rose E'er Blooming."

CHILD #2

What is that?

BARTHOLOMEW

It's a slow, dainty song that is sung delicately.

FILLMORE

Like this!

MUSIC CUE: FILLMORE kazoos, slowly, but humorous expressions on his face, "Lo, How a Rose E'er Blooming." CHILDREN laugh.

BARTHOLOMEW

(Interrupts FILLMORE'S kazooing.) Hey, stop! The Pastor is coming!

FILLMORE

Everyone hide your kazoos!

(Everyone, except BARTHOLOMEW, hides their kazoo. The PASTOR enters.)

1   PASTOR

2

3 *(Speaking in an accusatory way.)* Bartholomew! Is *that* a kazoo?

4

5   BARTHOLOMEW

6

7 Well, uh, yes, it is a kazoo, Pastor. Fillmore and I found them
8 in the Sunday School closets you told us to clean out.

9

10   PASTOR

11

12 So *all* of the children have kazoos? *(CHILDREN and FILLMORE bring*
13 *out kazoos.)*

14

15   BARTHOLOMEW

16

17 *(Looks down, embarrassed or in shame.)* Yes, Pastor, I gave them
18 all to the children.

19

20   PASTOR

21

22 *(Grabs stomach, as if sick.)* Oh, my, not me, too.

23

24   FILLMORE

25

26 Pastor, are you okay?

27

28   PASTOR

29

30 *(Hunched over.)* Oh, I am getting sick, too, and the pageant
31 starts in a few minutes!

32

33 *(Looks at BARTHOLOMEW.)* I was coming over to ask for your help.
34 The Organist told me you were starting a kazoo choir.

35

36   BARTHOLOMEW

37

38 Well, um… kind of?

39

40   PASTOR

41

42 Well, the Organist got really sick just a little bit ago.

43

44   *(Holds his abdominal area,*
45   *as if in pain.)*

46

47 And now I must be getting it, too!

48

49 *(Looks up, as if making a discovery.)* I *know* what it was.

50

51 *(In agony.)* We both ate some bad fruitcake!

1   CHILDREN
2
3 *Ewwww!*
4
5   FILLMORE
6
7 Is there a such thing as "good" fruitcake?
8
9   BARTHOLOMEW
10
11 *(To Fillmore.) Shhhh!*
12
13 *(To pastor.)* What can we do?
14
15   PASTOR
16
17 That's why I was looking for you, but now *I'm* sick, too.
18
19 *(Calls off-stage to ALISA.)* Alisa! Come here!
20
21   ALISA
22
23 *(Walks in, and sees PASTOR hunched over.)* Hello… oh, Pastor! Are
24 you okay?
25
26   PASTOR
27
28 *(Struggling, sick.)* Alisa… I am really sick…
29
30   FILLMORE
31
32 *(Interrupts.)* Fruitcake.
33
34   *(Looks at BARTHOLOMEW*
35   *and nods in agreement.)*
36
37   BARTHOLOMEW
38
39 *Bad* fruitcake.
40
41   PASTOR
42
43 *(Struggling, sick.)* I need *you*, Alisa, to do the lessons for the
44 Christmas Eve pageant…
45
46   ALISA
47
48 *(Interrupting.)* Yes, I can do that for you.

1   PASTOR

     (Struggling, sick.) And I need you, Bartholomew and Fillmore, to *save* the Christmas Eve pageant.

                                                ALISA

     What?

                                                PASTOR

                 (Hunching over, struggling and
                 sick, PASTOR begins to walk off
                 stage.)

     I need the three of you to conduct the lessons and the pageant.

     (Looking at the kids.) And all of you kids, I need you to give us a "Kazoo Christmas!"

                                             FILLMORE

                 (As PASTOR leaves stage,
                 FILLMORE calls to him.)

     I hope you feel better!

                                        BARTHOLOMEW

     (Hesitatingly, calling PASTOR.) Merry… *Christmas?*

                                                ALISA

     "Merry Christmas!" Who says that to a sick Pastor?

                                        BARTHOLOMEW

     Well… that was unexpected.

                                             FILLMORE

     Yeah, we went from hijacking the pageant to *being* the pageant.

                                                ALISA

     I can't believe this.

                                      BARTHOLOMEW

     Oh, this will be the greatest Christmas pageant ever!

1 (Looking at the children.) I mean, the greatest "Kazoo
2 Christmas" ever!
3
4   CHILDREN
5
6 Yay! (Children cheer and kazoo, and may exit the stage.)
7
8   BARTHOLOMEW
9
10   (Approaches ALISA.)
11
12 Alisa, it's time for you to un-harden your heart…
13
14 (Pauses.)
15
16 To worship with a kazoo.
17
18   (BARTHOLOMEW offers ALISA
19   a kazoo.)
20
21   ALISA
22
23
24   (Raises hands, and steps back
25   From BARTHOLOMEW's kazoo.)
26
27 I still can't believe this.
28
29   FILLMORE
30
31 Yeah, it will be a miracle if we pull this off!
32
33   (ALISA accepts the kazoo from
34   BARTHOLOMEW.)
35
36   BARTHOLOMEW
37
38 Well, Christmas is a time for believing in miracles!
39
40   (Looks at audience, mischievously.)
41
42 …A kazoo Christmas miracle!
43
44
45 End of Act III.

1
2
3

<u>MUSICAL INTERLUDE 3</u>

4 MUSIC CUE: "O Come, O Come Emmanuel" on kazoos, children and
5 audience invited, led by Bartholomew and Fillmore. The song is
6 kazooed slowly and mysteriously, but in a humorous way.

ACT IV

TIME: The present.
Christmastime.

PLACE: A church sanctuary.

ALISA is standing in a
pulpit. The CHILDREN are
outside of the sanctuary,
in costume for a nativity
pageant.

ALISA

The first lesson.

In the beginning was the word, and the word was with God, and
the word was God.

This pageant is our celebration of the coming of the Word into
the world.

MUSUC CUE: One verse of "O Little Town of Bethlehem" on
kazoos, children and audience combined, led by BARTHOLOMEW and
FILLMORE.

> *(During the song, children costumed*
> *as MARY and an ANGEL walk onto*
> *stage and take position in a nativity*
> *scene.)*

ALISA

The second lesson.

When Mary was a young girl, the angel Gabriel came to visit
her, and said, "Behold, the Lord is with you. You are carrying
a child, and you will name him Emmanuel, which means 'God with
us.'"

Mary responded, "Let it be with me according to your word,"
and she sang a song of thanksgiving for everything God has
done for the world, and especially for what God is about to do
in the world.

MUSIC CUE: One verse of "Angels from the Realms of Glory," on kazoos, children and audience combined, led by BARTHOLOMEW and FILLMORE.

> *(During the song, MARY exits*
> *or stands to the side, and JOSEPH*
> *enters, sitting or lying down,*
> *asleep, with the ANGEL standing*
> *next to him.)*

                              ALISA

The third lesson.

Joseph, a carpenter from Nazareth who was engaged to Mary, is visited by an angel in a dream. Joseph is told that God has created a miracle inside of Mary, and that the baby Jesus would arrive soon.

MUSIC CUE: One verse of "What Child is This," on kazoos, children and audience combined, led by BARTHOLOMEW and FILLMORE.

> *(During the song, the Angel exits*
> *and the KING enters, standing in a*
> *high position, pointing as if making*
> *an order. Nearby MARY enters,*
> *pregnant, standing with JOSEPH,*
> *as if they are walking.)*

                              ALISA

The fourth lesson.

The King called for a census to be taken and everyone had to return to their hometowns.

Along the way, Mary knew she was ready to have the baby.

Joseph guided Mary into the small village of Bethlehem, to look for a place to stay.

MUSUC CUE: One verse of "The First Noel" on kazoos, children and audience combined, led by BARTHOLOMEW and FILLMORE.

> *(During the song, the KING exits,*
> *and MARY and JOSEPH enter a*

1   *manger, surrounded by one or more*

2   *ANIMALS.)*

3

4

5   ALISA

6

7 The fifth lesson.

8

9 Joseph and Mary stop in Bethlehem and, looking for a place to

10 stay, they find nowhere to go. An innkeeper offers them his

11 manger for the couple to sleep.

12

13

14 MUSUC CUE: One verse of "We Three Kings" on kazoos, children

15 and audience combined, led by BARTHOLOMEW and FILLMORE.

16

17   *(During the song, three MAGI, a*

18   *child dressed as a STAR, and the*

19   *KING enter. The Magi appear as*

20   *if they are walking with gifts to*

21   *Mary and Joseph, and the KING*

22   *and STAR stand behind them to*

23   *the right and left.)*

24

25

26   ALISA

27

28 The sixth lesson.

29

30 Magi in the East studied the stars looking for signs from God,

31 and a dazzling star appeared to the West, and they left their

32 homes searching for the great new thing God is doing in the

33 world.

34

35 They brought with them on their journey gifts of gold,

36 frankincense, and myrrh.

37

38 Along the way, they are intercepted by the King, who was

39 looking for Jesus to harm him.

40

41 MUSUC CUE: One verse of "Hark! The Herald Angels" on kazoos,

42 children and audience combined, led by BARTHOLOMEW and

43 FILLMORE.

44

45   *(During the song, SHEPHERDS*

46   *and ANGELS enter and take their*

47   *places around the nativity scene.)*

ALISA

The seventh lesson.

While shepherds were keeping watch outside of Bethlehem, a host of angels appeared spectacularly and brilliantly in the sky!

The Angel of the Lord spoke: "I bring you tidings of great joy, for unto you a child is born in the City of David. Go, and you will find a baby in a manger, which will be a sign for you."

The glorious multitude of angels sang: "Glory to God in the highest, and peace on earth, and good will toward all!"

MUSIC CUE: One verse of "Angels We Have Heard on High" on kazoos, children and audience combined, led by BARTHOLOMEW and FILLMORE.

> (During the song, a BABY
> JESUS appears with Mary).

ALISA

The eighth lesson.

Then the miracle happened: *Jesus is born!*

When the shepherds arrive to the manger, the immediately bowed down to worship the baby Jesus, knowing that he is a sign of peace to the common people.

The shepherds spread the news what had happened: what the angel told them and that they found Jesus, just as the angels said they would.

Mary held the newborn Jesus and pondered all these things in her heart.

MUSIC CUE: One verse of "Away in a Manger" on kazoos, children and audience combined, led by BARTHOLOMEW and FILLMORE.

BARTHOLOMEW

(Whispering loudly.) Kids, here's the big moment!

MUSIC CUE: One verse of "Silent Night" on kazoos, children and audience combined, led by BARTHOLOMEW and FILLMORE.

FILLMORE

(With relief.) I can't believe we pulled that off!

ALISA

Fillmore, um… we're still in the pageant!

FILLMORE

(Looks out into audience, shocked.)

Oh. Well, I guess we didn't think how we end the pageant. What would the Pastor do right now?

ALISA

I don't know, would the Pastor preach?

FILLMORE

(Gestures his hand and his neck, as if to say, "Cut it short.")

Or … give a benediction?

BARTHOLOMEW

(Walks into the pulpit or wherever the Pastor would be speaking.)

(Clears his throat.) Good morning, church!

I have a confession to make. We were going to hijack the Christmas Pageant with these kazoos we found in the back of the Sunday School classroom closets.

But when the Pastor asked us to take over the Pageant, I know that God is working in mysterious ways…

(Pauses.)

… in mysterious *kazoo* ways.

And God gave us all gifts this Christmas, and sometimes we need to be nudged to open them.

(Looks to the audience.)

Can I get an "Amen," church?

> *(All yell, "Amen!")*

ALISA

(Astonished.) Bartholomew, that was beautiful.

FILLMORE

Wait a minute…

(Points to back of audience.)

…is that the organist sneaking around back there?

BARTHOLOMEW

It can't be, she's sick.

ALISA

(Looking.) I think it is!

ORGANIST

> *(The ORGANIST enters, and walks*
> *from the back or side of the stage or*
> *sanctuary.)*

Yes, it is me!

FILLMORE

I thought you were sick!

ORGANIST

Nah! When I heard you were putting together a *coup d'état* of the Christmas pageant, I figured, if you wanted to do the Christmas pageant, why don't you just ask?

ALISA

So *you* were behind this?

ORGANIST

Yep. I knew you could do it.

(Thinking while speaking.) I'm thinking that I can take an Easter off for the first time in 300 years, since you all are capable of leading worship and music without me and the Pastor.

FILLMORE

Hold on, where is the Pastor?

ORGANIST

       (Walks toward organ or piano.)

He had some bad fruitcake. He wasn't looking so good; he was as green as a Christmas tree.

BARTHOLOMEW

Well, I sure hope he feels better!

       (Pauses, then makes some notes on
       his kazoo to get everyone's attention.)

There is only one thing left for us to do.

ALISA

What's that?

FILLMORE

I know! "Joy to the World!"

BARTHOLOMEW

Let's do it!

MUSIC CUE: One verse of "Joy to the World" performed joyfully on the organ and kazoos, with BARTOLOMEW and FILLMORE leading the kazooing.)

1   BARTHOLOMEW
2
3   Merry Christmas everyone!
4
5
6   *End of Act IV.*
7
8

APPENDIX

ADVENT CANDLE LIGHTINGS

to be used in conjunction with the pageant.

Advent 1

Reader: We light the first candle to pray for hope.

               Hope is what Jesus brings into the world: hope for the future, hope for the children, and hope for the nations as we await his arrival.

               We hope that the church maintain and tend this fire in our hearts, that, against all odds, the future arrives.

The first candle is lit in silence.

Song: "O Come, O Come, Emmanuel," one verse, respectfully and reverently on the kazoo or the kazoo with other instruments.

Advent 2

Reader: We light the second candle to pray for peace.

               Peace is brought into the world with the baby in a manger.

               Jesus teaches us the difference between the peace which is defined by the nations and the peace which God alone can offer:

               The peace which is the end of divisions between peoples, families, communities, and countries.

               The peace which is freely offered to us in the promise of our salvation.

               The peace that we live when we cease to be possessed by our possessions.

The first two candles are lit in silence.

Song: "O Come, O Come, Emmanuel," one verse, respectfully and reverently on the kazoo or the kazoo with other instruments.

Advent 3

Reader: The third candle is lit as we pray for joy.

We make joyful noises in our worship, and sometimes we hold back.

When we pray for joy we pray that Jesus unlocks our hearts and our spirits to worship without obstacles.

When we pray for joy we live the experience of Christ being born in us and deliver hope, peace, joy, and love into our homes, our work, or schools, and our relationships.

When we pray for joy we seek a glimpse of the healing of the trees of nations promised to us when God's children are finally and truly one.

May our joy be driven by a desire for unity.

Three candles are lit in silence.

Song: "O Come, O Come, Emmanuel," one verse, respectfully and reverently on the kazoo or the kazoo with other instruments.

Advent 4

Reader: The fourth Advent candle represents love.

There are many different kinds of love. The love of God is the most mysterious and difficult to understand of all.

God's love for all of God's children presented to us in the coming of the Son in the manger.

God's love is also given to us in the church as a challenge to lure is into a new understanding and practice of love that is expansive, beyond any conception of mercy, and is baffling to logic or reason.

As we light the fourth candle, let love be kindled in our hearts but more importantly, may love be practiced and instigated by words and our hands.

The four candles are lit in silence.

Song: "O Come, O Come, Emmanuel," one verse, respectfully and reverently on the kazoo or the kazoo with other instruments.

Christmas Eve

Reader: We have been waiting through the cold of winter for a rose to blossom.

We have been waiting, praying for hope for the impossible to be made actual.

The first candle is lit.

We have been waiting amidst wars and rumors of wars, hearing the principalities and powers assure us that there is peace, when there is no peace.

But peace is not only possibility, but nurtured in the waters of the womb.

The second candle is lit.

We have been waiting from dark and deep places, from pits and watery turbulence, in grief and in depression, to have the experience of joy announced to each of us, and to the world.

The third candle is lit.

We have been waiting for love to arrive to us, the love which transcends life and death, the love which is beyond all understanding. The love which offers and models forgiveness.

The fourth candle is lit.

In the bleakest of times God shatters into the world to be with us, to live with us, and to lure us into a being a church which both celebrates the wonderful news of the Christ who is born in a manger and being a church that follows that child to the cross.

The Christmas candle is lit.

Song: "O Come, All Ye Faithful," one verse, joyfully and in celebration on the kazoo or the kazoo with other instruments.

NOTES

NOTES

Barber's Son Press

York, Pennsylvania

Ingram Content Group UK Ltd.
Milton Keynes UK
UKHW051005050623
422889UK00012B/1463